COOKING AGAINST THE GRAIN: *Sweet Revenge*

Orleatha Smith, HLC

ISBN: 1480280747
ISBN-13: 978-1480280748

⚠ CAUTION

This book, while grain free, by no means intends to say that the treats contained herein are "healthy".

They ARE healthier than processed, grain-filled, junk food and, MUCH tastier!

Please enjoy these treats responsibly.

This book is dedicated to my husband's grandfather Clinton Oliver Irvine because he loved to bake and was one of the kindest, sweetest men I will ever have the pleasure of meeting. Forever in my heart.

Jamaica
2004 (above)
2012 (at Right)

My Story

At 5'4 my highest recorded weight, I was 258 pounds. That was the weight taken at my annual physical with my general practitioner – who was at least 300 pounds himself. The doctor came in with the results of my bloodwork. My thyroid hormones were out of whack, my blood pressure was elevated and to top it off, my stroke number was 5 times higher than it should have been -- All at the ripe old age of 30.

I wasn't sure how he could help me but I felt that I had run out of options. I had been to Weight Watcher six (yes six) times. I had tried EVERY other diet and I was tired, and sick. I decided to have Roux N Y gastric bypass.

I had to go through a series of meetings and consultations and, after having a million pre-tests run I had my surgery on 4/21/ 2009. Over the course of a year, I lost 90 pounds of my excess weight. I was steady at 165 pounds. I had more energy than I had at 258 (who wouldn't). I also started to watch the scale start to creep up. Instantly, I reverted back to my old ways – my diet mentality kicked in. I counted every calorie, gram of fat, ounce of carbs. I lost a pound, gained two; I lost two pounds, gained one back. Had I gone through ALL of that only to gain it back? Would I be banished to a life of low fat micro-meals and calorie counting?? I ended up gaining almost 20 pounds back in my efforts to lose weight – again.

After some convincing from friend who resolved her own PCOS with Paleo and switched her entire family to the Paleo lifestyle, I decided to give it a try. The first week was hard but by the second week, I felt a burst of energy that I hadn't felt in what seemed like YEARS. At the end of 30 days, I stepped on the scale and discovered that I had lost 15 pounds! In addition to seeing the scale move, I also witnessed:

- My skin has cleared up –WITHOUT the use of corticosteroids!
- My hormones are back in check.– and not a cramp in sight.

Paleo (ancestral, traditional, holistic, whatever you want to call it) is sustainable. I can do this forever. It really is as simple as eating real foods - eliminating processed crap. Other diets and plans were not really sustainable for me because they relied on frozen this or that, or I had to go to a meeting or I had to eat boring food and starve the rest of the day!

Paleo also taught me to listen to my body. If I am eating a boat-load of protein and start to feel lethargic then maybe it's my body saying "Hey, I don't like that" so I should back off. If I'm hungry, I eat. If I'm not, I don't. It is so super simple and I think that's what makes it complicated for some.

I have evolved so much in the last few years! I am empowered to make the best decisions for my life and not others. Along the way, I've found that I have to do what is right for me – without regard for what other people think. I've started a wellness company to help other people on their journey and have completely changed my career goals!

For the first time in my life I'm okay with being different. I don't mind telling people (kindly) that I won't be partaking in their feasts consisting of standard American diet foods. I ask a million questions at restaurants. I now have a local farmer and hit the farmer's market every week for my organic veggies and pastured eggs.

A final word about those who might be considering gastric bypass
I completely empathize with those who are considering surgery! I know the shame associated with it all too well. Some refer to gastric bypass as 'the easy way' – it is not! It's the hardest thing I have ever done.

The first year is the sweet-spot for weight loss – after that, the body starts to return to normal. At the two year point, you will likely be able to eat whatever you could before you had surgery. If you have not changed your mindset, you will gain the weight back. Of course no surgeon will ever tell you this…

Surgery is a weight-loss tool – not a health-gaining tool. My advice: Find a sustainable health-gaining program and do that instead. I recommend Paleo (ancestral, traditional, holistic, whatever you want to call it).

Coconut Flour

Coconut flour doesn't work the same as grain-based flours like wheat or rice in baking. This makes baking with it a bit of a challenge. I'm always up for a challenge so let's look at a few tips and tricks to make your treats come out wonderfully!

What is it?

Coconut flour is a soft, fine powder produced from dried coconut meat. It is a natural byproduct of coconut milk production. When coconut milk is pressed from coconut meat, bits of solid coconut are leftover. This leftover meat is then dried at a low temperature and ground until it produces a soft flour. It offers a gluten-free, protein-rich alternative to grain-based flours. It can be made at home but to save time and effort, I typically purchase my coconut flour in bulk online. Here are some sources for coconut flour:

> Tropical Traditions
> Bob's Red Mill
> Edward & Sons Trading Co (Let's Do Organic)
> Honeyville Grain
> More Than Alive
> Wilderness Family Naturals
> Nuts Online

Why?

* **Filling**
  Rich in protein, fiber and fat makes coconut flour very filling.
* **Immune system and Thyroid support**
  Coconut flour is rich in lauric acid. Lauric acid, a saturated fat, is thought to support the immune system, the thyroid and also promotes good skin health.
* **Great source of manganese**
  Manganese helps your body utilize many nutrients including choline and biotin (found in eggs), vitamin C and thiamin. Manganese also supports bone health, nervous system function, and thyroid health as well as helps to maintain optimal blood sugar levels.

The Scoop

* Coconut flour and grain based flours are not equal. They cannot be substituted on a one-to-one ratio
* Coconut flour is very absorbent so little coconut flour is needed to successfully produce a recipe.
* Coconut flour is dense and can also be dry. Be sure to use enough eggs or pureed fruit to ensure that your baked goods come out deliciously moist.
* Allow coconut flour to soak for about 15 minutes after mixing it in with the liquid ingredients. This will make the final textured product much moister and less grainy.
* SIFT your flour. Since coconut flour is clumpy and so dense, even the most carefully taken measurement can be thrown off if coconut flour is not properly sifted.

Almond Flour

What

Almond flour is simply ground almonds. It lends a slightly sweet and nutty flavor to the dish, without being overbearing. There are different types of almond flour.

Blanched

Blanched almond flour makes the best textured baked goods. The finer the grind, the better. It is made by steaming almonds to remove the skin of the almonds before grinding. The nuts are then dehydrated and finely ground, resulting in very fluffy, light and airy flour.

Almond Meal

Almond Meal is simply ground almonds made with the whole almond, skins and all. It is usually coarser. It is great to give a cornbread texture to baked goods and is great for breading on chicken, fish and more.

Like coconut flour, I typically purchase my almond flour in bulk online. Here are some sources for almond flour:

> Hughson Nut, Inc.
> Honeyville Food Products
> Lucy's Kitchen Shop
> Amazon.com
> SunOrganic Farm
> Digestive Wellness
> Bob's Red Mill Almond Meal/Flour
> Buy Almond Flour
> Benefit Your Life
> NutsOnline
> JK Gourmet

Almonds bought in the U.S. are not "truly" raw. Most have been pasteurized to some degree. These online stores (and others) offer truly raw nuts and nut flours.

> The Raw Food World
> Living Nutz: Truly RAW and organic nuts.

The Scoop

Tips

- ✸ Low and Slow. Almond flour, like all nut flours, burns easily. Be sure to keep the temperature low and be prepared to bake longer than you would if using a grain-based flour. Since all ovens heat differently, be sure to check your baked goods about mid-way through to be sure they aren't burning.

- ✸ Buy in bulk if you plan on baking a lot. Almond flour can get expensive, but most websites you order from will give you a discount if you buy in bulk. You can store the flour in your refrigerator

---

for a month and your freezer for around 6-8 months. If you store in your freezer, just remove the portion you need for your recipe and let thaw at room temperature for 30 minutes.

✱ Almond flour can rarely be used on a 1:1 ratio because its weight, fat content and absorption rates are so different from that of wheat and other grain based flours. It does not reliably cross over in grain-based recipes.

A final word on alternative flours

When using alternative flours, it is always best to weigh instead of using a measuring C for reliable results. Digital scales are widely available and affordable. Many people are intimidated by the idea of weighing their ingredients, but in reality it is really easy and creates a consistent product. Here's how to make the conversion:

Almond Flour

1 C	3.5 ounces
½ C	1.6 ounces
¼ C	0.8 ounces

Coconut Flour

1 C	4 ounces
½ C	2 ounces
¼ C	1 ounce

Double Chocolate Chip Cookies

Swet Potato Brownies

Sunbutter Bon Bons

Butter Cookies

Cookies and other hand-held goodies

Choco Mint Cookies

Chocolate Chip Almond Butter Cookies

Makes: About 24 cookies

Ingredients

1 C almond butter

1/4 C coconut oil

1/4 C raw honey

1 egg

1 tsp vanilla extract

2 C almond meal

¼ C semi sweet soy-free chocolate chips

1/2 tsp baking soda

Directions

Preheat oven to 350 degrees. Line a baking sheet with parchment paper

In a large bowl, stir together almond butter, coconut oil, and honey. Beat in egg and vanilla extract

In a small bowl, combine almond meal, chocolate chips, and baking soda. Stir dry ingredients into wet ingredients and mix well

Scoop the dough 1 Tbsp at a time and roll into balls. Set the balls on the baking sheet and flatten

Bake for 10 -12 minutes, until the edges just start browning

Soft Baked Chocolate Chip Cookies

Makes: About 24 cookies

Ingredients
½ C coconut oil, melted
2 tsp vanilla extract
4 eggs, room temperature
½ c coconut milk

½ c maple syrup
1 C coconut flour
¼ tsp sea salt
¾ C soy-free chocolate chips

Directions
Preheat oven to 350 degrees. Line a baking sheet with parchment paper
Combine all wet ingredients
Add coconut flour and sea salt mixing well to combine then fold in chocolate chips
Scoop and form 2 inch balls
Flatten onto parchment lined baking sheet
Bake for 15-20 minutes or until golden brown

Soft Sunbutter Cookies

Makes: About 24 cookies

Ingredients

1/4 C coconut oil, melted
2 tsp vanilla extract
4 eggs
½ C coconut milk
½ C maple syrup
1 C coconut flour

¼ tsp sea salt
¼ tsp baking soda
½ C sunbutter
¼ C almond butter
2 Tbsp coconut sugar

Directions

Preheat oven to 350 degrees. Line a baking sheet with parchment paper
Combine all wet ingredients
Add coconut flour and sea salt mixing well to combine
Scoop and form 2 inch balls
Flatten onto parchment lined cookie sheet
Bake for 15-20 minutes or until golden brown

Sweet Potato Brownies

Ingredients

12 medjool dates, pitted
1 C mashed sweet potato
3 eggs
½ C pastured butter, melted
2 tsp vanilla extract
3 Tbsp coconut flour

½ C unsweetened cocoa powder
¼ tsp baking soda
½ tsp cream of tartar
2 Tbsp fine coffee grounds
½ C soy-free chocolate chips

Directions

Preheat oven to 350 degrees and grease a 9x13 glass baking dish

Soak dates in warm water for about 10 minutes

Drain then place the medjool dates in a food processor and pulse until completely pureed

Add mashed sweet potato and process until pureed and combined with the dates

Add mixture to the bowl of a stand mixer, add the eggs, vanilla extract, and butter until well combined

In a separate bowl, combine the coconut flour, cocoa powder, baking soda, cream of tartar and coffee grounds

Slowly add the dry ingredients into the wet ingredients and mix on low-speed, scraping down the sides, until you have a smooth batter

Fold in chocolate chips

Pour in the batter and smooth it with the back of a spatula

Bake for 30-35 minutes or until a toothpick stuck in the middle comes out clean.

Bacon Brownies

Ingredients

4 oz unsweetened chocolate, melted in 1 T
Coconut Oil

2 large avocados

½ C raw honey

3 eggs

¼ C unsweetened cocoa powder

1 Tbsp vanilla extract

1 Tbsp coconut flour

1 tsp baking soda

½ tsp sea salt

Topping

1 3.5 ounce 80% chocolate bar (like Green &
Black's)

1 Tbsp coconut oil

5 strips crisp bacon, chopped

Directions

Preheat oven to 350 degrees and grease a 8x8 glass baking dish

Puree the avocado flesh in a food processor until completely smooth

Beat remaining wet ingredients together with the avocado in a bowl

Add in dry ingredients and beat until fluffy

Spoon batter into baking dish

Bake at for 35 minutes, or until a toothpick comes out smooth

Once cooled, melt chocolate bar with coconut oil, mix well then spread a thin layer over brownie

Sprinkle with chopped bacon and let harden in refrigerator

Banana Choco Cookies

Makes: About 24 cookies

Ingredients

2 bananas, thoroughly smashed
1/3 C coconut flour
½ tsp salt
3/4 C almond butter
½ tsp baking soda

1/3 C dark chocolate chips
1 apple finely chopped
1/3 C coconut milk
1 Tbsp cinnamon

Directions

Preheat oven to 350 degrees. Line a baking sheet with parchment paper
In a medium mixing bowl, add the bananas, coconut flour, almond butter, and baking soda and mix well
Fold in the chocolate chips, apples, coconut milk, and cinnamon then mix in remaining ingredients
Scoop out dough into heaping tablespoons onto the parchment paper, placing an inch or two apart
Bake for 25 minutes

Double Chocolate Chip Cookies

Makes: About 24 cookies

Ingredients
¼ C chopped dates

2 Tbsp water

4 eggs

¼ C raw honey

1 tsp vanilla extract

½ C pastured butter, melted

1 C coconut flour

¼ C unsweetened cocoa powder

¼ tsp sea salt

¾ C dark chocolate chips

Directions
Preheat oven to 350 degrees. Line a baking sheet with parchment paper

Pulse water and dates in a food processor until jelly-like, scraping down sides as necessary

Wisk eggs, honey, vanilla extract, and butter together

Add in cocoa powder and coconut flour

Using a spatula, mix in chocolate chips

Scoop out dough into heaping tablespoons then shape into cookies

Bake for 15 minutes

Shortbread Cookies

(Courtesy of PaleoSpirit)

Makes: About 24 cookies

Ingredients

1 C coconut flour
1/2 C arrowroot starch/flour
1 C coconut oil or ghee or butter, melted
2/3 C maple syrup

1 Tbsp vanilla extract
1/2 tsp cinnamon
1/4 tsp sea salt

Directions

Preheat oven to 350 degrees. Line a baking sheet with parchment paper
Place all ingredients in a large bowl and combine using a fork to make sure everything is evenly distributed.
Press the dough together to make a solid piece
Turn out the "dough" onto a large piece of parchment or wax paper
Form a log then, using a sharp knife, cut ½ inch squares
Transfer cookies to parchment paper lined baking sheet bake for 15 minutes.
Once the shortbread cookies have cooled slightly you can move them to a wire rack.

Butter Cookies

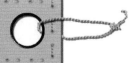

Makes: About 24 cookies

Ingredients
2 C almond flour
¼ C coconut flour
½ tsp sea salt
¼ C raw honey

½ C cold pastured butter, cut into small pieces
1 tsp vanilla extract

Directions
Preheat oven to 350 degrees. Line a baking sheet with parchment paper
In a large bowl, whisk dry ingredients together
Add honey, butter and vanilla extract
Use your hands to combine ingredients until they form small crumbs. It should stick together if you pinch some between your fingers
Place crumbly dough on parchment paper then place another piece of parchment paper on top
Roll the dough into a long rectangle then use a knife or pizza cutter to cut the rectangle into 2 inch bars
Use a spatula to transfer the bars to a parchment lined cookie sheet
Bake for 12 minutes or until the edges are lightly browned

Sunbutter Bon Bons

Makes: About 24 bon-bons

Ingredients

20 dates, pitted
1/2 C almond butter
1/2 C sun butter
1/3 C coconut oil

2 Tbsp raw honey
1 Tbsp coconut flour
2 Tbsp almond flour
10 oz soy free chocolate chips

Directions

In your food processor, puree the dates into a paste
Add almond butter, sunbutter, coconut oil, coconut flour almond flour and honey and pulse until smooth
Add mixture to sauce pan and cook over medium-low heat until it just starts to bubble
Place in refrigerator for 30 minutes until it is cooled to room temperature
Scoop and form into balls
Chill for 60 minutes or until very stiff
Melt chocolate in double boiler
Coat each ball in chocolate and set on wax paper and chill in the refrigerator to harden chocolate

Choco-Mint Cookies

Makes: About 24 cookies

Ingredients

1 C almond flour
1/4 C coconut flour
1 egg
1/2 tsp sea salt
¼ C unsweetened cocoa powder

3 Tbsp raw honey
2 tsp peppermint extract
2 Tbsp avocado oil
coconut oil

Cookie coating

8 ounces dark chocolate (over 60%)

2 tsp peppermint extract

Directions

Preheat oven to 350 degrees. Line a baking sheet with parchment paper
Mix all ingredients together until you can form a ball
Oil your hands with coconut oil
Using the dough, form 1-inch balls then flatten into discs
Place on parchment paper and bake for 15 minutes or until discs look dry

After cookies have cooled, place dark chocolate in small sauce pan over medium heat stirring until melted
Remove from heat, add peppermint extract to melted chocolate and stir
Dip cookies in mint chocolate and place on wax paper
Let chill in refrigerator to harden

Pineapple Upside Down Cake

Chocolate Layer Cake with Chocolate Frosting

Cakes and other utensil-needy fare

Pineapple Upside Down Cake

Ingredients

4 eggs
½ C crushed pineapple
2 Tbsp apple cider vinegar
½ C coconut milk
½ C raw honey
½ C + ½ C pastured butter, melted
1 Tbsp vanilla extract

1 C coconut flour
½ tsp baking soda
1 tsp sea salt
1/4 C coconut sugar
1 20-ounce can pineapple slices in juice, drained well
butter for greasing pan

Directions

Preheat oven to 350 degrees. Grease 1 9-inch round cake pan with butter

Beat the eggs with the coconut milk, ½ c butter, vinegar, honey and vanilla extract, until smooth.

Add the crushed pineapple, coconut flour, baking soda and salt mixing until a smooth batter forms. Divide the coconut sugar evenly into each pan. Pour the remaining melted butter equally over the coconut sugar swirling to make sure the bottom of the pan is evenly covered. Arrange the pineapple slices over the coconut sugar

Bake for about 20 minutes then lower the temperature to 325 degrees and continue baking until cake separates from the sides of the pan and a toothpick inserted into the center comes out clean.

Allow to cool about 15 minutes before inverting the cakes onto wire racks to cool completely.

A note about Maraschino cherries

Maraschino cherries were originally soaked in 70-proof Maraschino cordial made from the juice of the Italian Dalmatian marasca wild cherry. I decided to leave them out because today, the commercial maraschino cherries we know are put into a brining liquid of sodium metabisulfate, calcium chloride, and citric acid; soaked in corn syrup and fructose solution, then artificially flavored and colored. Really makes you think twice about them, doesn't it?

Apple Pie

Ingredients

Crust:

1 1/2 C almond flour

1/2 C coconut flour

1 Tbsp raw honey

1/2 tsp salt

1/2 C pastured butter, cold

6-9 Tbsp ice water

¼ C coconut sugar

Filling:

4-5 granny smith apples, peeled and sliced

1 Tbsp cinnamon

3 Tbsp raw honey

1 Tbsp vanilla extract

1 tsp sea salt

2 Tbsp arrowroot

Directions

Preheat oven to 325 degrees

In bowl, combine crust ingredients except butter and water

Using a pastry cutter or two knives, cut butter into crust to form pea size clumps

Mix in ice water, a few tablespoons at a time, until crust forms and will hold together between your fingers, but is not sticky

With 3/4 of the crust, form in the bottom of a greased pie plate with your fingers. This crust is very delicate, so it will be difficult to transfer if you roll it out.

Once crust is formed, mix together filling ingredients and pour into crust

Add the coconut sugar to the remaining 1/4 crust mixing well to create crumble topping. Cover pie with topping then place in for 35-40 minutes.

Banana Bread – Nut Free

Ingredients

4 ripe bananas, mashed
1/4 C pastured butter, melted
6 eggs
1 Tbsp vanilla extract
3 Tbsp maple syrup
1/2 C coconut flour

1/2 tsp baking soda
1/4 tsp cream of tartar
2 Tbsp arrowroot
1/4 tsp sea salt
1 Tbsp cinnamon

Directions

Preheat oven to 325 and grease loaf pan with butter
Combine all dry ingredients then set aside
Whisk eggs until frothy then add bananas, butter, vanilla extract and maple syrup
Add dry ingredients to wet making sure to mix well then pour into loaf pan
Bake 50-60 minutes or until toothpick inserted into the center comes out clean

Banana Bread

Ingredients

3 bananas (about 1½ cups) mashed

3 eggs

1 Tbsp vanilla extract

1 Tbsp cinnamon

½ Tbsp nutmeg

1 tsp ground ginger

2 Tbsp honey

¼ C butter or coconut oil

2 Cs blanched almond flour

½ tsp sea salt

1 tsp baking soda

Directions

Preheat oven to 350 and grease loaf pan with butter

Combine bananas, eggs, vanilla extract, honey and butter in a bowl

Pulse in almond flour, cinnamon, nutmeg, ginger, salt and baking soda

Spoon batter into a greased loaf pan, smoothing out the top

Bake for 55-65 minutes or until toothpick inserted into the middle comes out clean

Banana Pudding

Ingredients

Custard

¼ C maple syrup
1 Tbsp arrowroot
1/4 tsp salt
5 egg yolks
2 14oz cans coconut milk

3 Tbsp butter or coconut oil divided
2 tsp vanilla extract
3 VERY ripe bananas mashed
3 ripe bananas - whole

Cookies

Shortbread cookies, pg 17

Directions

Bring first 5 ingredients to a boil in a heavy saucepan over medium heat (about 20 minutes), whisking constantly until thickened.
Remove from heat. Stir in butter and vanilla extract.
Place 1 Tbsp of butter in medium sized skillet over medium heat
When butter is melted, add mashed bananas
Cook for 5 minutes to caramelize bananas then add to custard.
Use a hand mixer to puree custard and bananas; Can also add half of the custard and all of the bananas to a food processor until liquefied.
Pour into bowl then place heavy duty plastic wrap directly on surface of custard to keep "skin" from forming.
Chill at least 2 hours

While custard is chilling, make shortbread cookies
Layer short bread cookies, bananas and pudding mixture in a glass serving bowl.
Repeat until all custard, cookies and bananas are used. Chill until serving.

Bananas Foster Ice Cream

Ingredients

1 Can (14 0z) coconut milk [preferably first press]
2 egg yolks
1 Tbsp melted grass fed salted butter
1/8 tsp sea salt

2 Tbsp rum
1 tsp cinnamon
½ Tbsp molasses
1 Tbsp Raw Honey
3 ripe bananas

Directions

Blend all ingredients in a food processor or blender until smooth

Pour into ice cream maker and let go for 45 min; alternatively you can pour into glass or stainless steel container and freeze for 3 hours

Since this recipe uses alcohol the end product will be softer and that it will take longer to freeze as alcohol lowers the freezing point of anything it's added to

Transfer it to a glass or stainless steel bowl and serve if you like it soft, or put in freezer for an additional 30 minutes or longer for desired consistency

Chocolate Layer Cake with Chocolate Frosting

Ingredients

Cake

1 C coconut flour

3/4 C cacao powder

1 tsp baking soda

1 tsp sea salt

9 eggs

3/4 C pastured butter, melted

1 C Tbsp maple syrup

1 C strongly brewed coffee

2 Tbsp vanilla extract

Coconut oil and parchment paper for pans

Frosting

1 ½ C heavy whipping cream, very cold (preferably raw)

2 Tbsp maple syrup

1 Tbsp coconut oil, melted

4 ounces dark chocolate

1 tsp vanilla extract

Pinch of sea salt

Directions

Preheat oven to 325 degrees and grease 2 9-inch round pans

Line the bottom of each pan with parchment paper

Beat eggs until frothy then mix in other wet ingredients

Mix dry ingredients in a small bowl

Add the dry ingredients to the wet ingredients mixing well until batter is fluffy

Divide the batter between the two pans

Bake for about 40 minutes until cake separates from the sides of the pan and a toothpick inserted into the center comes out clean

Allow the pound cake to cool before removing it from the pan

For the frosting:

Melt chocolate in a double boiler then stir in oil, maple syrup and salt. Remove from heat.

Pour cream and vanilla extract into a bowl then whisk using a standing mixer with a whisk attachment or a regular hand mixer until cream starts to thicken and hold a stiff peak

When chocolate has cooled, gently fold the chocolate into the whipped cream

Use this between layers of the cake and as frosting

Buttery Pound Cake

Ingredients

5 eggs

½ C coconut milk

½ C honey

½ C pastured butter, melted

1 Tbsp vanilla extract

1 C coconut flour

½ tsp baking soda

1 tsp sea salt

butter for greasing pan

Directions

Preheat oven to 325 degrees and grease fluted Bundt pan

Beat eggs with the coconut milk, honey and vanilla extract, until smooth

Add the coconut flour, baking soda and salt mixing until a smooth batter forms

Pour batter into the Bundt pan

Bake for about an hour or until pound cake separates from the sides of the pan and a toothpick inserted into the center comes out clean

Allow the pound cake to cool before removing it from the pan

Chocolate Orange Cake

Ingredients

1C coconut milk

3 eggs

½ C raw honey

½ C organic cocoa powder

1 Tbsp vanilla extract

½ tsp baking soda

¼ tsp sea salt

Zest from 1 orange

½ C almond flour

Directions

Preheat oven to 325 degrees and grease an 8x8 pan

Place all of your dry ingredients together in a mixing bowl then mix

Add wet ingredients and use your hand mixer and form your batter

Pour your batter into the prepared pan

Bake for 30-35 minutes or until a toothpick inserted into the middle comes out clean

Grain Free Cinnamon Rolls

Ingredients

Dough
3 C almond flour
½ C golden flax meal
¼ C coconut flour
1 1/2 tsp baking soda
1/4 tsp salt

1 tsp cream of tartar
3 large eggs
1/3 C raw honey
¼ C coconut milk

Filling
2 Tbsp pastured butter, melted
1/3 C raw honey
4 dates, pitted

¼ c coconut sugar
1 Tbsp cinnamon

Directions
Preheat oven to 325 degrees and grease an 8x8 pan

Dough:
In a bowl combine the dry ingredients.
In a separate bowl, combine the wet ingredients.
Add dry ingredients to wet ingredients until well combined and dough is formed

Filling: Mix all ingredients in a food processor until smooth.

Oil an 18 inch sheet of parchment paper with coconut oil
Generously oil your hands with coconut oil then place the dough on the oiled parchment paper
Press the dough into a 1-inch thick rectangle
Spread the filling mixture evenly all over the dough
Using the parchment paper, roll the dough up into a tight spiral then gently peel paper away
Using a long piece of plain dental floss slice the roll into 2-inch rolls
Place the rolls into the prepared pan side by side
Brush on a little more melted butter or oil on to the tops
Place into the oven and bake 20-25 minutes

Vanilla Custard

Ingredients

¼ C maple syrup
1 Tbsp arrowroot
1/4 tsp salt
5 egg yolks

2 14oz cans coconut milk
3 Tbsp pastured butter or coconut oil divided
2 tsp vanilla extract

Directions

Bring first 5 ingredients to a boil in a heavy saucepan over medium heat (about 20 minutes), whisking constantly until thickened
Remove from heat and stir in butter and vanilla extract.
Pour into bowl then place heavy duty plastic wrap directly on surface of custard to keep "skin" from forming
Chill at least 2 hours

Flourless Mint-Chocolate Cake

Ingredients

10 Tbsp pastured butter

2 tsp peppermint oil

12 oz 85% dark chocolate (like Green & Black's)

6 eggs, room temperature

1/4 C pure maple

Directions

Preheat oven to 350 degrees and grease an 9-inch round pan

In a double boiler, melt chocolate then add in butter until smooth

Remove from heat then mix in peppermint oil

In a stand mixer, beat the eggs and syrup on high for 7-10 minutes, until light and fluffy

Turn the mixer to low and slowly add in the melted chocolate mixture until all the chocolate is incorporated

Fill half way a roasting pan or other pan with sides at least 1-1/2 to 2 inches high with hot water

Pour into greased cake pan and place the cake pan into the roasting pan

Bake for about 45 minutes, until the top begins to look "dull" but isn't cracking.

Remove from oven and cool

S'Mores Pie

Ingredients

Crust
3 1/2 Cs almond flour
1 tsp baking soda
1 Tbsp cinnamon
7 Tbsp coconut oil, chilled
2 Tbsp vanilla extract

5 Tbsp coconut milk
1/2 C honey
¼ tsp baking soda
½ tsp cream of tartar

Marshmallows
1/3 C honey
1/2 C cold water, divided
2 packets unflavored gelatin

1 egg white
1 tsp vanilla extract

Directions
Dissolve the unflavored gelatin in ¼ cup cold water in a heat-proof bowl
Heat honey and remaining water in saucepan on medium-high heat stirring until dissolved
Insert a candy thermometer and heat mixture until it reaches 240 degrees
While honey mixture is heating, whip egg white until soft peaks form
Once honey mixture reaches 240 degrees, pour it into gelatin water and stir to combine then add vanilla extract
Allow to cool for 3-4 minutes, then pour mixture in a steady stream into whipped egg white, whipping to until stiff peaks form

Combine almond meal, baking soda, and cinnamon in bowl or food processor
Add in coconut oil and combine until you reach a coarse meal
In a separate bowl, whisk together vanilla extract, coconut milk and honey, add to the almond meal mixture and combine well.
Press half of dough mixture into 9-inch cake pan then top with broken chocolate bar then marshmallow
Roll the remaining dough between two sheets of parchment paper
When dough is about 1/4 inch thick, peel off the top layer of parchment paper
Invert onto prepared pie pan
Bake 20 minutes, until slightly brown

Lemon Squares

Ingredients

Crust

1 ¾ C almond meal

½ tsp baking soda

2 Tbsp pastured butter

1 Tbsp vanilla extract

2.5 Tbsp coconut milk

¼ C raw raw honey

1/8 tsp baking soda

¼ tsp cream of tartar

Filling

4 egg yolks

1 C raw honey

¾ c lemon juice from 6 to 7 lemons

3 Tbsp arrowroot

1 Tbsp tapioca starch

Directions

Preheat oven to 350 degrees and grease a 9x7 pan

Combine dry ingredients in bowl or food processor

Add in butter and combine until you reach a coarse meal

In a separate bowl, whisk together vanilla extract, coconut milk and honey

Add to the almond meal mixture and combine well

Drop dough onto a piece of plastic wrap, form into a ball and wrap completely

Refrigerate for an hour or until firm

Once dough is firm press into bottom of prepared pan

Bake in a 350 degree oven for 15-25 minutes, until slightly brown. Cool completely

Reduce oven temp to 300 degrees

For the filling:

In a large bowl, whisk together all ingredients

Pour the filling into the prepared crust

Place the dish in the center of the oven and bake until custard is set, about 40 minutes

Cool to room temperate then cut and serve

Cinnamon Crunch Cereal

Ingredients

1 C almond meal
1 C chopped almonds
1 C flax meal
½ C coconut flour
2 Tbsp coconut oil
2 egg whites
2 Tbsp maple syrup

4 Tbsp raw honey
2 tsp vanilla extract
2 tsp cinnamon
1 tsp nutmeg
1 tsp salt
4 dates, finely chopped

Directions

Preheat oven to 275. Combine almond meal, flax meal, coconut flour, cinnamon, nutmeg, salt and chopped almonds. In a separate bowl, combine coconut oil, egg whites, maple syrup, raw honey, vanilla extract and chopped dates. Add coconut oil mixture to almond meal mixture. Thoroughly combine taking care not to break down larger 'nuggets'. Spread mixture on ungreased baking sheet. Bake for 90 minutes stirring every 30 minutes. Cool and store in an airtight container.

Waffles

Cinnamon Buns

Garlic Cheddar Biscuits

Pancakes

Biscuits, Rolls, and other yummies

Easy Cheesy Rolls

Garlic Cheddar Biscuits

Ingredients

6 eggs
¼ C pastured butter, melted
1/2 C coconut milk
1/2 C coconut flour
1/4 tsp baking soda

½ tsp cream of tartar
2 cloves of garlic, pressed
1 C shredded sharp cheddar
1 tsp parsley
¼ tsp sea salt

Directions

Preheat oven to 350 degrees and grease 6 large muffin tins

Whisk eggs then mix in garlic, coconut milk and melted coconut oil or butter

Mix in coconut flour, parsley, baking soda, cream of tartar & salt until blended

Fold in shredded cheddar

Fill each of the oiled muffin tins with ½ C of mixture

Bake for approximately 30 minutes or until the muffins are set and edges begin to become golden brown

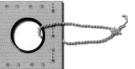

Waffles

Ingredients

4 eggs

4 Tbsp pastured butter
2 Tbsp maple syrup
1 Tbsp vanilla extract
1/2 C water
3 C almond flour
1 tsp sea salt
1 tsp baking soda
1 Tbsp cinnamon
2 Tbsp arrowroot
1 C apple sauce

Directions

In a medium bowl, whisk together wet ingredients, until smooth

In a separate bowl, combine the almond flour, salt, baking soda, arrowroot powder, and cinnamon

Add almond flour mixture to egg mixture and combine thoroughly

Spoon into heated waffle iron

Cook until steam slows from waffle iron and waffles are golden brown

Pancakes

Ingredients

4 eggs
1 C coconut milk
1 Tbsp vanilla extract
1Tbsp maple syrup
1 Tbsp cinnamon

1/2 C coconut flour
1/2 tsp sea salt
1 tsp baking soda
2 tsp apple cider vinegar
Coconut oil for frying

Directions

In a small bowl mix wet ingredients

In a separate medium-sized bowl whisk together dry ingredients

Stir wet mixture into dry until everything is incorporated

Melt butter/ coconut oil in a skillet over medium heat

Ladle a few Tbsp of batter into pan for each pancake spreading them out slightly with the back of the spoon

Cook for about 2 minutes until the tops dry out slightly and the bottoms start to brown. Flip and cook an additional 2-3 minutes

Sweet Potato Biscuits

Ingredients

2 eggs

1/4 C butter, melted

1 Tbsp raw honey

1/2 C sifted coconut flour

2 Tbsp arrowroot

1/4 tsp salt

1/4 tsp baking soda

½ tsp cream of tartar

1 ½ C mashed sweet potato

Directions

Preheat oven to 350 degrees and line a cookie sheet with parchment paper

Whisk eggs then mix in remaining wet ingredients

In a separate bowl, mix dry ingredients then add wet ingredients to dry

Spoon ¼ cup of the mixture onto parchment paper shaping into biscuits

Bake for approximately 20 minutes or until the biscuits are set and edges begin to become golden brown

Cinnamon Buns

Ingredients
1 C tapioca flour
½ tsp cream of tartar
¼ tsp baking soda
2 Cs mozzarella cheese, grated
3 large egg yolks

2 Tbsp raw honey
1 Tbsp cinnamon
2 to 3 Tbsp coconut milk
Coconut oil

Directions
Preheat the oven to 350 degrees and line a baking pan parchment paper
Combine the tapioca flour cream of tartar, cinnamon, and baking soda together in a large bowl
Stir in the cheese, honey, and egg yolks
Oil your hands with coconut oil and knead the dough with your hands until the dough is smooth and even-textured
If the dough doesn't come together or seems too stiff, then add coconut milk, 1 tablespoon at a time, until it comes together and feels supple
Divide the dough into 10 even pieces and with your hands, roll each into a ball
Shape the balls into ovals and place them 1-inch apart on the prepared baking sheet
Bake until the rolls are golden, about 15 to 20 minutes.
Cool on a wire rack for 5 to 10 minutes and serve while still warm

Easy Cheesy Rolls

Ingredients

1 C tapioca flour, plus extra for kneading
½ tsp cream of tartar
¼ tsp baking soda
1 C mozzarella cheese, finely grated

1 C Italian cheese blend (such as asiago, parmesan, etc.)
3 large egg yolks
2 to 3 Tbsp coconut milk

Directions

Preheat the oven to 350 degrees F. Line a baking pan parchment paper
Combine the tapioca flour cream of tartar, and baking soda together in a large bowl
Stir in the cheeses and egg yolks
Knead the dough with your hands until the dough is smooth, even-textured, and not sticky
If the dough doesn't come together or seems too stiff, then add coconut milk, 1 Tbsp at a time, until it comes together and feels supple
Divide the dough into 10 even pieces and with your hands, roll each into a ball
Shape the balls into ovals and place them 1-inch apart on the prepared baking sheet
Bake until the rolls are golden, about 15 to 20 minutes
Cool before enjoying

27125019R00026

Made in the USA
Lexington, KY
28 October 2013